A Family in Mexico

This book takes you on a trip to bustling Mexico City, one of the largest and most crowded cities in the world. There you will meet the Marmalejo family. Odilon Marmalejo is a silversmith and he will show you how he turns lifeless metal into beautiful ornaments. You will also discover what the rest of the family do, what they like to eat, and what their hobbies and interests are.

FAMILIES AROUND THE WORLD

A FAMILY IN
MEXICO

Peter Otto Jacobsen and
Preben Sejer Kristensen

The Bookwright Press
New York · 1984

Families Around the World

A Family in France
A Family in Mexico
A Family in India
A Family in Holland

First published in the United States in 1984
by The Bookwright Press, 387 Park Avenue South, New York, NY 10016

First published in 1984 by
Wayland (Publishers) Limited
49 Lansdowne Place, Hove
East Sussex BN3 1HF, England
© Copyright 1984 Text and photographs
Peter Otto Jacobsen and
Preben Sejer Kristensen

© Copyright 1984 English-language edition
Wayland (Publishers) Limited

ISBN 0–531–03787–8
Library of Congress Catalog Card Number: 84–70781

Printed in Italy by G. Canale and C.S.p.A., Turin

Contents

Flying to Mexico   6
By taxi to Mexico City   10
We meet Odilon Marmalejo   12
Mexican silverware   14
Where the Marmalejos live   18
The Marmalejo family   20
Family life   24
Mealtime   26
Facts about Mexico   30
Glossary   31
Index   32

Flying to Mexico

We are flying to Mexico, the third largest country in Latin America, from Guatemala, a smaller country to the south. Far below us are the tropical jungles and grasslands of the state of Chiapas, where noisy parrots and macaws, toucans and hummingbirds abound. Caymans (a kind of alligator) infest the rivers and lagoons, while at night vampire bats fly in search of cattle's blood to drink.

Much of the southeastern part of Mexico is covered by dense jungle.

Oil, which is drilled from the sea bed under the Gulf of Mexico, is the country's most valuable resource.

Through the airplane window, we can just see, to our right, the blue sea of the Gulf of Mexico. Here, oil rigs of the state-owned oil company, Pemex, drill for oil in the shallow waters around the coast. Oil is Mexico's most valuable resource and makes up about one-third of all her exports.

With an area of 1,972,000 sq. km. (761,600 sq. mi.), Mexico is the third largest country in Latin America.

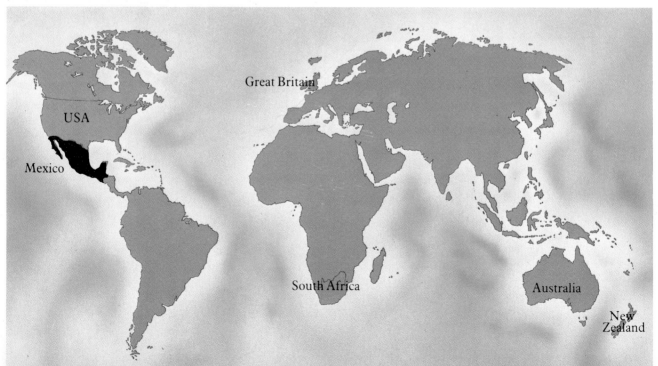

As the airplane turns to land at Mexico City airport we can marvel at the two huge volcanoes that overshadow the city – Mt. Popocatapetl and Mt. Ixtaccihuatl – both of which are more than 5,000 m. (17,000 ft.) high. The mountains were named by the Indians, who were the only people living in Mexico until the Spanish arrived in the sixteenth century. The Indians say that when Popocatapetl rumbles, he is mourning for his dead sweetheart, Ixtaccihuatl.

The volcano, Mt. Popocatapetl, was given its name by the Mexican Indians called Aztecs.

The mountains continue north of Mexico City and later divide into two ranges – the Sierra Madre Occidental ("occidental" means western) and the Sierra Madre Oriental ("oriental" means eastern). On the high plateau between the mountains are thousands of tiny farms, where corn, wheat and grapes are grown, and pigs, sheep and cattle are raised.

Mexico's capital, Mexico City, is one of the largest cities in the world.

Here, too, there are many silver mines. Mexico is one of the world's largest producers of silver, and soon we will meet a man whose job it is to turn the silver into beautiful ornaments, bowls, plates and other items.

9

By taxi to Mexico City

We fight our way through the usual airport bustle and wait for a taxi to take us into Mexico City itself. The air is quite cool; temperatures never rise much over 25°C (77°F) because the city is more than 2,000 m. (7,000 ft.) above sea level.

The journey to the city center is only five kilometers (three miles) long, but it seems to take an age. This is not surprising in a city of about fourteen million people and two million vehicles. The traffic on the broad main streets frequently comes to a standstill and our driver shouts angrily, and waves his fist at the pedestrians who step straight out in front of us. We soon realize why Mexico City has one of the highest accident rates in the world!

All around, tall buildings reach up almost to the sky. The giant Latin American Tower in the central plaza, the Zocala, is the highest building in Mexico. Also in the plaza is the beautiful cathedral, which was begun in 1573 and took 250 years to complete.

The cathedral in the main square.

10

Eventually, we turn down a side street, past stalls selling freshly-squeezed fruit juices or tortillas. These are rolled up pancakes filled with chillies, tomato sauce or grated cheese. We stop outside the firm of Tane and Co., where Odilon Marmalejo works as a silversmith.

An old man watches us as we speed past. Behind him is the giant Latin American Tower.

We meet Odilon Marmalejo

Odilon greets us like old friends with an *abrazo*. This is the traditional Mexican bear hug, and it almost takes our breath away. Then he shows us into the small smithy where he is foreman. About a dozen men are busy making trays, animals, bowls and dishes from large sheets of silver.

Odilon is 38 years old and has been working with silver for twenty-three years. Both his father and his grandfather before him were silversmiths.

Odilon Marmalejo has been a silversmith since he was 15.

"My father taught me everything I know," he says. "I worked long hours and was paid only a few pesos a week, but I couldn't have had a better teacher. Even now, I still work sixty hours a week, from

Odilon proudly shows us some of the silverware he has made.

9 o'clock in the morning until 9 o'clock at night. But now I am paid much better wages," he adds, grinning broadly.

13

Mexican silverware

Odilon shows us how he and his men fashion the silver. It is all done by hand, and the hammer is the most important tool. The sheets of silver are cut with hacksaws to the required size and heated with a gas-fired torch. Pots and dishes are shaped over cast-iron "heads" which fit into a bench vice. It is a wonderful sight to see the silversmiths turning the lifeless shiny metal into beautiful and useful objects.

Silver animals are among the most popular products of the Tane and Company silver smithy.

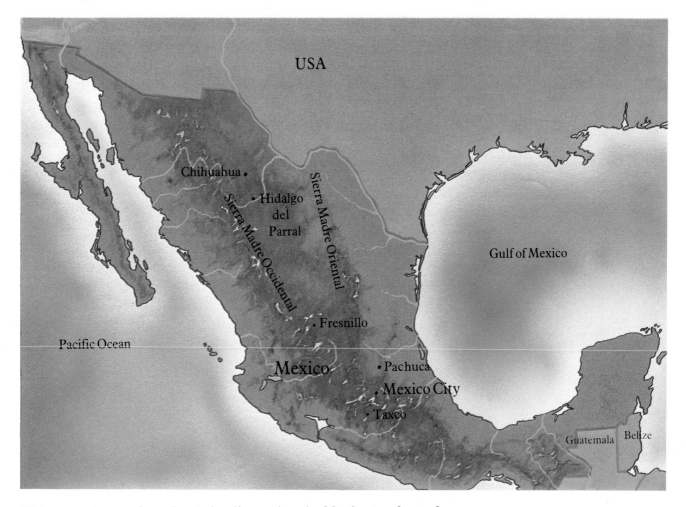

This map shows where the main silver mines in Mexico are located.

"Our silver arrives here from mines in the Pachuca district, about ninety-five kilometers (sixty miles) northeast of here, and from near the cities of Chihuahua, Fresnillo and Hidalgo del Parral and near Taxco," Odilon tells us.

"Silversmithing is a very ancient craft, in Mexico," he goes on. "The Indians were great craftsmen. But the tradition had all but died out until about fifty years ago. Then, an American, called William Spratling, revived the craft in Taxco. Today, that town is world famous for its silverware, and one in every four people is employed in the industry. But the items they make are mainly for the tourist trade. I think our silverware is much better."

Silver is not the only mineral found in Mexico. Gold is mined and so are zinc, lead and sulphur. Mexico is also a leading producer of mercury, cadmium and manganese.

After Odilon has shown us around the smithy, it is time to drag ourselves outside and into the traffic once more. Odilon has taken the afternoon off work to introduce us to his wife and family. He takes one look at the idle traffic and throws his arms up.

"It will take us hours to get home through this," he says.

One of Odilon's most valuable tools is the gas-fired torch.

Odilon uses a bench vice to hold this silver horse while he carefully shapes the head.

Where the Marmalejos live

Odilon and his family live in a suburb some fifteen kilometers (nine miles) from the smithy.

We wait patiently in the slow-moving traffic. Above the roar of engines and hooting of car horns, Odilon tells us something about the city in which he has spent all his life.

"Mexico City was founded by the Spanish Conquistadores who came here in the sixteenth century," he says. "It was built on the same site as the ancient Aztec City of Tenochtitlan. Archaeologists are still finding valuable remains of the old city right beneath our feet."

Eventually, after nearly an hour's journey we arrive in the suburbs. The Marmalejos live in a lovely, white, two-story house. There is a small garden in the front with a green lawn and flowers. As soon as we step into the living room we are left in no doubt but that this is the house of a silversmith.

The living room in the Marmalejos' home is crowded with silverware.

The low table is covered with silver ashtrays and other ornaments. On the shelves in another room, there are more beautiful items – cups with swan's heads as handles; copies of Aztec figures; cigarette boxes of braided silver thread; and many, many more.

Two of the most beautiful ornaments in Odilon's house are these swan-shaped cups.

The Marmalejo family

Odilon's wife, Adela, greets us warmly, and hands us a cup of steaming Mexican coffee. Then she begs us to sit down.

Like ten percent of all Mexicans, the Marmalejos are pure-blood Spanish. Two-thirds of all Mexicans are *mestizos*. This means that they are part-Spanish and part-Indian. The proportion of true Indians is about thirty percent and falling rapidly.

Adela is a housewife, but apart from her duties in the home she has many hobbies.

"I love macramé," she says, showing us the hanging baskets she has made for her plants. "I also bowl and paint."

Both the Marmalejo children go to the local elementary school. Like most schools in Mexico it is run by the state and is free. José will be leaving elementary school to go to secondary school when he is 15. Later, he has been promised, he will go to London for a year to improve his English.

Adela uses her skills at macramé to make lovely hanging baskets for her plants.

20

Adela sends both of her children to the local state school.

"It is very important for Mexican children to speak good English," says Adela, "because so much of Mexico's trade and business is done with the United States."

José loves sports, and keeps himself fit by weightlifting.

In his spare time, José engages in sports.

"I love basketball, tennis and swimming," he says, "but soccer is my favorite. It's the number one sport in Mexico. Papa often takes me to watch the international matches at the Aztec stadium here in Mexico City."

Mariana is a little shy and cuddles up close to her father. Although she is only 8, she can already speak a little English. She doesn't know what she wants to be when she grows up, but José has already

The Aztec Stadium where Odilon takes José to watch international soccer matches.

made up his mind. He is going to be an engineer.

23

Family life

Mariana is learning English at the local elementary school.

Odilon likes to keep himself fit by jogging and shadow boxing. He does all the work outside the house – the gardening and the painting.

"Washing, cleaning, cooking and all the work inside the house Adela takes care of," he says. "We share the work that way."

Neither José nor Mariana have any particular duties in the home. They help out when they are asked to, but homework takes up much of their time.

"We get up at about 7 o'clock on most mornings," says Adela. "For breakfast we usually have cereal, eggs, coffee and some fruit. Odilon leaves for work at about 8 o'clock and the children go to school at about the same time," she goes on. "Then I can get on with the housework."

24

"Traditionally, Mexican families have always been very close-knit," says Odilon, "but recently this seems to be changing. Now nearly one in three marriages in Mexico ends in divorce, and family life is threatened."

Adela begins telling us about *Movimiento de Encuentros Conyugales*. This is an association which tries to strengthen the ties in Mexican families.

"Both Odilon and I are members of the association," she says. "It's made up of sixty groups working all over Mexico."

"Every two weeks we hold meetings in our group to discuss and plan out our activities," says Odilon. "They include, among other things, holding lectures telling people how best to protect the family."

"I hope that we can bring Mexican families together again," says Adela as she returns to the kitchen to put the finishing touches to our evening meal.

Adela is cooking for us the family's favorite meal – fillet of beef Mexican style.

Mealtime

Adela does most of her shopping in the modern supermarkets, many of which are supported by the government to keep prices down. But for fresh fruit and vegetables she prefers the traditional markets where you can still haggle over prices.

Tonight, because we are special guests, Adela is cooking for us the family's favorite dish – home-made pea soup, followed by boneless beef Mexican style. This is beef cooked in a special sauce with mushrooms and bacon.

Although there are plenty of supermarkets in Mexico, Adela prefers shopping in the local market.

Mexican beef cooked in a special sauce.

As we sit down to dine, the whole family says grace together. Like most Mexicans, the Marmalejos are staunch Catholics and attend Mass regularly.

"We were married at the local church fifteen years ago," says Adela. "We actually met for the first time at a party. Odilon kissed me but he didn't propose to me right away as he should have done. I had to wait some time for him to propose," she adds, looking at her husband and smiling.

Adela and her husband are very happy together, and they like to show it even when other people are around. There is no doubt that it really upsets them to see so many Mexican families breaking up.

"Our dream," says Odilon, "is that we will grow old together, and live as long as possible."

"But first and foremost," says Adela, "we believe that our children should be happy."

"We think that the future looks very bright," says Odilon. "Although Mexico is going through an economic crisis now, I'm sure we'll get over it. The only thing we really fear is the destruction of family life," he adds. "We prize family life most of all."

We thank the family for the meal and leave the table to go. Odilon insists that we take some small silver ornament with us to remind us of our day with the Marmalejo family.

Odilon and Adela agree that the most important thing in their lives is that their children should be happy.

Facts about Mexico

Size: The area of Mexico is about 1,972,000 sq. km. (761,600 sq. mi.).

Capital city: The capital of Mexico is Mexico City.

Population: About 62,500,000 people live in Mexico.

Language: Ninety-five percent of all Mexicans speak Spanish, but there are also five Indian languages.

Money: Mexicans pay for things in pesos and centavos. There are 100 centavos in a peso. A peso is worth about 0.55 US cents.

Religion: There is no official religion in Mexico but most people are Roman Catholics.

Climate: The climate in Mexico is different in different parts of the country. In some places it is hot, rainy and tropical; in other places it is rainy but cooler; and in some areas it is dry desert.

Government: Mexico is a federal republic. It has a president who is elected every six years.

Education: Mexican children go to elementary school from ages 6–14 and to secondary school from ages 15–19.

Agriculture: The main products from the farms in Mexico are corn, beans, rice, wheat, sugar cane, coffee, cotton, tomatoes, chillies, tobacco, chickpeas, peanuts, sesame, alfalfa, cocoa, and many kinds of fruit. Even the cactus is used to make drinks like tequila.

Industry: Mexico is rich in minerals and in oil and natural gas. The main minerals are gold, silver, copper, lead, zinc, iron, mercury and sulphur.

Glossary

Aztecs Mexican Indian people who ruled over a huge empire until it was overthrown by the Spanish Conquistadores in the sixteenth century.

Bench vice A tool which is fixed to a bench and has two movable jaws which can hold things tightly.

Cadmium A light-colored metal which is used in the generation of nuclear power.

Chillies Small red pods of a plant. They are used for flavoring meat dishes, pickles and sauces.

Conquistadores The Spanish adventurers who conquered much of Central and South America in the sixteenth century.

Corn A cereal crop with large ears of yellow seeds. There are several varieties, such as Indian corn and sweetcorn.

Latin America The areas of Central and South America and the Caribbean where Spanish or Portuguese is the main language spoken.

Macramé The art of knotting and weaving coarse thread into shapes and patterns.

Manganese A greyish-white metal used in making steel.

Propose To make an offer of marriage to someone.

Index

Aztecs 8, 18

Chiapas 6

Family life 24–5
Farming 9, 30
Food and drink 10, 26

Indians 8, 16, 18
Ixtaccihuatl, Mt. 8

Jungles 6

Latin American Tower 10, 11

Marmalejo family 20, 24–5
  Adela 20
  José 20
  Mariana 23
  Odilon 12–18
Marriage 25, 27
Mestizos 20
Mexico City 8, 10–11
Minerals 16, 30

*Movimiento de Encuentros
  Conyugales* 25

Oil 7, 30

Pemex 7
Popocatapetl, Mt. 8

Religion 27, 30

Schools 20, 30
Shopping 26
Sierra Madre Occidental 9
Sierra Madre Oriental 9
Silver mining 9, 14–15, 30
Silversmithing 12–17
Sports 22, 23

Taxco 16
Tenochtitlan 18
Tortillas 10

Wildlife 6

Zocala 10

Acknowledgements

All the illustrations in this book were supplied by the authors, with the exception of the following:
Bruce Coleman (Jaroslav Poncar) 6; John Topham 8, 26, Syndication International 23. The maps
on pages 7 and 15 were drawn by Bill Donohoe.